THE
ONE
A Christmas Devotional

Thank you to Brenda Vann, Michael Maginness, and Greg Shawgo for their help in proofreading this work. I am forever grateful for their counsel, encouragement, and expertise in completing this project.

Introduction

Every Christmas we hear the same saying, "Jesus is the reason for the season." This statement is very true, and I agree with it one hundred percent. However, what do we mean when we say this? It is one thing to say it; however, a completely different thing to act upon it. What does a Christmas centered on Christ look like—a Christmas that is more than just traditions, sentimentalities, and gift giving? I am not opposed to any of these wonderful and beloved aspects of celebrating Christmas. However, I fear that many believers confuse the worship of Christ with the traditions that this special holiday brings.

It must be noted that the Bible doesn't command or even suggest that we celebrate Christmas. However, one cannot go wrong with a dedicated period of time that is focused on biblical truth.

That is what I have sought to do in this brief devotional. My desire is to direct your hearts to Christ. These devotionals are very doctrinal as they focus on Christology (The study of Christ) as we seek to answer the question, "Who is Jesus?" Doctrine matters in all seasons and Christmas is no exception.

I am not asking you to set aside your traditions associated with Christmas. I am asking you to quietly devote a few minutes over the next twenty-five days to focus on the truth of Jesus' deity, humanity, and purpose for coming. My prayer is that after you complete these readings that you will treasure Christ more. May we be people who treasure Christ apart from Christmas traditions. May we worship His glory more than the goods that come our way. May we pray, reflect, and store these things up in our hearts, not just for this season, but for the days and months, and years to come.

I pray these devotionals will whet your appetite for the beauty, majesty, and glory of Christ. I have prayerfully written these devotionals so that those who know Him might be more fully sanctified in their faith. I have also considered those who may not even know Christ in a saving way. May the Lord be with you all as you read and worship the Christ of Christmas with rich doctrinal truth.

This is the One. Merry Christmas!

December 1st

The One Who Is Himself a Gift

Thanks be to God for his inexpressible gift!
2 Corinthians 9:15

Christmas is the time of year when we give gifts to others to remember the birth of Jesus. At least that's the way it's supposed to be, right? Oftentimes, we are very preoccupied about getting just the perfect gift. Sometimes these gifts leave our loved ones speechless and sometimes it's just the "thought that counts." There is a great joy in the act of giving a gift.

I have received some wonderful gifts from some wonderful people. However, none of them can compare to the gift given by the ultimate gift giver, God. God is the ultimate giver and cannot be outgiven. *"Every good gift and every perfect gift is from above…" (James 1:17)* We receive daily gifts from God even though we may not even realize it. Each morning we breathe, taste, smell, drink, and our hearts pump blood through our bodies. It's the simple things that don't even come across our minds that are gifts to us. I believe sometimes we feel that we are owed these things. However, God is under no obligation to give us anything at all.

Everything that we have is because of His grace and mercy.

Of all the gifts that we have received from the Lord, there is One that stands above them all. Paul describes this gift as "inexpressible" in his second letter to the Corinthians. The context of this verse is Paul encouraging the Corinthians to give towards the work of the ministry. He wanted them to give willingly and cheerfully (2 Corinthians 9:7). He motivates them by using God as the example of how they ought to give. The inexpressible gift is the grace of God displayed to us in the Lord Jesus. God didn't send money, cars, gadgets, or even toys our way. Neither did He give us what we wanted. Instead, He gave us what we needed. What we thought we wanted before we knew we needed Jesus was just more sin. He gave us Jesus, and He did so willingly, sacrificially, and gladly.

The gift of Jesus to us is an inexpressible treasure. He gave us *"his only Son."* May we truly understand that in Christ we have been given a gift that no human words can fully describe. Paul is correct in that the gift of Jesus is inexpressible. God's gift to us should humble us and truly leave us speechless. Charles Spurgeon preached the following in a sermon, "A man who has received a gift, and never looks at it, and never thanks the giver, will come by degrees to forget that he has it, or to forget the giver, and to forget how he came by it. Cultivate a grateful spirit when you think of what a gift you have in Christ. Praise the Lord for Christ. Then you will want to praise Him again; and when you have praised Him again, you will want to praise Him yet again; and the more you praise Him, the more sure you will be that He is really yours."[1]

As we begin the month of December, let us pause to thank God for His inexpressible gift! God planned this gift before the ages began. (Ephesians 1:3-11) He doesn't give it because He wants to impress us; He gives it because He truly loves us. He knows exactly what we need. We need Jesus. We need the One who is Himself a gift.

This is the One. Merry Christmas!

---

[1] https://www.spurgeon.org/resource-library/sermons/gods-unspeakable-gift/

December 2ⁿᵈ

The One Who Is the Last Adam

Just as we have borne the image of the man of dust, we shall also bear the image of the man of heaven.
1 Corinthians 15:49

On the sixth day of creation, God made a man from the dust of the ground. Although this man was from the dust, he was made in the image of God (Genesis 1:27). This meant that this man was a walking reflection of who God was in his person. This man was not God, but the imprint of God's image was embedded in this man's being. The Hebrew word for man is âdam. This word is transliterated in the English for us as Adam.

Adam was to obey all of God's commands for this was God's world. Adam and his wife Eve disobeyed God and were cursed as a result of their rebellion. The penalty for their sin against God was death. They were no longer perfect reflections of God's image. That reflection was now marred by a darkness called sin and in God there *"is no darkness at all."* (1 John 1:5) Not only would Adam and Eve die but their offspring would die as well. Paul explains, *"Therefore, just as sin came into the world through one man, and death through sin, and so death*

spread to all men because all sinned." (Romans 5:12)
Therefore, all who come from Adam (every
human who has ever lived) sin by nature and are
deserving of death. It is no wonder that the world
is the way it is. It is a never-ending cycle of sin and
death, and it all began with Adam.

Why do we celebrate Christmas? We celebrate
Christmas because, through the incarnation of
Jesus Christ, God reversed the curse of Adam's
disobedience. The eternal Son of God took on
Adam's flesh and became a human. He was not
just human; He was also divine. However, being
born a man, Jesus did what Adam was supposed to
do — obey God. He did not just obey His Father
as a Divine being, but He obeyed God in Adam's
flesh, in Adam's place. Jesus was not just born to
die; He was also born to fulfill all of God's law
through perfect obedience.

Because we are born from Adam, we are
sinners who are under God's judgment and will
one day die. We are counted to be just as
disobedient as Adam. However, through the last
Adam, Jesus Christ, all who are born again are
under God's grace and mercy. Although they
physically die, they will live. We are counted to be
just as obedient as Jesus even though we aren't.
This is the true wonder of Christmas. Our physical

birth binds us to the disobedient Adam. Our spiritual birth binds us to the obedient Christ. Paul explains, *"Therefore, as one trespass led to condemnation for all men, so one act of righteousness leads to justification and life for all men. For as by the one man's disobedience the many were made sinners, so by the one man's obedience the many will be made righteous." (Romans 5:18-19)*

Jonathan Edwards writes, "Christ, the second Adam, acts the same part for us that the first Adam was to have done, but failed. He has fulfilled the law and has been admitted to the seals of confirmed and everlasting life. God, as a testimony and seal of His acceptance of what He had done as the condition of life, raised Him from the dead, and exalted Him with His own right hand, received Him up into glory, and gave all things into His hands. Thus the second Adam has persevered, not only for Himself, but for us; and has been sealed to confirmed and persevering and eternal life, as our head; so that all those that are His, and that are His spiritual posterity, are sealed in Him to persevering life."[2]

---

[2] From Jonathan Edwards's (1703-1758) treatise "Concerning the Perseverance of Saints" in *Works* 3: 512-13 (reprint of the Worchester edition in four volumes). In the Banner of Truth edition.

This Christmas, may we reflect on the truth that the One born in Bethlehem, was the One who is the last Adam. He is the better Adam; the obedient Adam. The One who doesn't pass on death and curses but eternal life by faith in Him.

This is the One. Merry Christmas!

December 3rd

The One Who Is the Ancient of Days

But you, O Bethlehem Ephrathah, who are too little to be among the clans of Judah, from you shall come forth for me one who is to be ruler in Israel, whose coming forth is from of old, from ancient days. — Micah 5:2

The little town of Bethlehem is not the place where you would expect the Messiah to be born. Why not have the Messiah born in Jerusalem? Wouldn't that attract more attention to His arrival? It probably would, but that is not how God willed it to be. Through the prophet Micah, it was known that Bethlehem would be the place where the Messiah would be born. In this prophecy it is even said that Bethlehem is *"too little to be among the clans of Judah."* When Joshua led Israel to settle into the promised land, Bethlehem was so insignificant that it wasn't even listed as a town within the region of Judah. Isn't it just like God to choose the most unlikely place?

Although Bethlehem was counted as insignificant, it is still extremely important in the history of Israel. For one, it was the birthplace of King David. It does make sense that the Messiah, who was to be a descendant of David, would be born in the birthplace of David (1 Samuel 17:12). This connection to King David was important as people investigated the true identity of Jesus. The insignificance of Bethlehem reminds us of David's background as well. David was the insignificant younger brother who was overlooked to be the king by his family (1 Samuel 16). Even while he was king, David was rejected from the throne by his own son and people (2 Samuel 15-20). David would foreshadow the fact that the Messiah would be, *"despised and rejected by men, a man of sorrows and acquainted with grief."* (Isaiah 53:3) John tells us, *"He came to his own, and his own people did not receive him."* (John 1:10-11). The name of Bethlehem is also significant. The Hebrew word means "house of bread." Is it a coincidence that Jesus who is the Bread of Life (John 6:35) was born in the house of bread? I think not. The Lord purposely chose Bethlehem to be the birthplace of Jesus.

Micah prophesied not just where He was physically born, but also His eternal origin. The prophecy was that the Messiah *"is from of old, ancient of Days."* He is from ancient days. This Hebrew word can be translated as "everlasting" or in reference to eternity. The only other person who this description can apply to is God Himself. *"Are you not from everlasting, O LORD my God, my Holy One?" (Habakkuk 1:12)* Further biblical evidence is seen in the prophecy of Daniel. Daniel also saw "the son of man" (a reference to the Messiah) and said He had come to the Ancient of Days. *"I saw in the night visions, and behold, with the clouds of heaven there came one like a son of man, and he came to the Ancient of Days and was presented before him. And to him was given dominion and glory and a kingdom, that all peoples, nations, and languages should serve him; his dominion is an everlasting dominion, which shall not pass away, and his kingdom one that shall not be destroyed." (Daniel 7:13-14)*

Jesus is the long-expected Messiah who was born humbly in insignificant Bethlehem just as God had wanted. However, He wasn't *originally* from Bethlehem. He is from eternity past. He is eternal. He is the Ancient of Days.

This is the One. Merry Christmas!

December 4th

The One Who Is Our Peace

For to us a child is born, to us a son is given; and the government shall be upon his shoulder, and his name shall be called Wonderful Counselor, Mighty God, Everlasting Father, Prince of Peace. Of the increase of his government and of peace there will be no end, on the throne of David and over his kingdom, to establish it and to uphold it with justice and with righteousness from this time forth and forevermore. The zeal of the LORD of hosts will do this.
Isaiah 9:6-7

The world has longed for peace for a very long time. There is much strife from within every segment of society and also around the globe. Nations rise against nations. Evil people with evil motives only wish to foster and advance what is godless in this world. Will there ever be an end to it? The hope of Christmas is that yes, there will be an end to these days.

Isaiah was a prophet of the nation of Judah. Judah was also known as the Southern Kingdom of Israel during the days of Isaiah. When Isaiah penned these words, Judah had enemies all around them, including the Northern Kingdom of Israel. The King of Judah was Ahaz who faced an imminent threat from the Northern Kingdom of Israel when they joined forces with the country of Syria. God promised King Ahaz that He would be with Judah and that the Northern Kingdom of Israel and Syria would soon be defeated. (Isaiah 7:14-16) God promised them that through a child that He would be with them.

Isaiah's prophecy is quoted every Christmas. However, do we really know what it means? Who is this child that was to end all wars? It is the Messiah! Who is He? He is *"Wonderful Counselor, Mighty God, Everlasting Father, Prince of Peace."* This child would be extraordinary! King Ahaz had much to fear in his day, but a child was coming to end the worry of God's people. There was going to come a time when He who sat on the throne of David would deliver never-ending peace, justice, and righteousness. There was coming a child that would have a kingdom which no country or evil could destroy. This is what Israel had long awaited in the years of their tumultuous history. They were looking for the One who would end the complete and utter oppression by the enemy and bring peace on earth. The good news is that this child has already come!

Without Christmas, this promise would have no fulfillment. This promise came in the form of a child that WAS given to us. He would not fail. He would succeed. His name is Jesus and He is the Prince of Peace. There is coming a day in which there will be no need for a Department of Defense or Homeland Security. There is coming a day in which there will be no need for the White House, Congress, or any form of government. King Jesus will reign and when He does, He subjects all of His enemies under His feet. The promise is not just true for King Ahaz, but also for all of us who call upon His name.

This was the news the angels had for the shepherds on the night Jesus was born. *"And suddenly there was with the angel a multitude of the heavenly host praising God and saying, 'Glory to God in the highest, and on earth peace among those with whom he is pleased!'" (Luke 2:13-14)*

Not only would the Messiah bring peace on earth, but more importantly, He brings peace with God. *"Therefore, since we have been justified by faith, we* [a] *have peace with God through our Lord Jesus Christ." (Romans 5:1)* Jesus is our peace.

This is the One. Merry Christmas!

December 5th

The One Who Is the Branch

*There shall come forth a shoot from the stump of Jesse,
and a branch from his roots shall bear fruit.—Isaiah 11:1
(see also Jeremiah 23:5; 33:15; Zechariah 3:8; 6:12)*

The nation of Judah escaped the threat of war
with the Northern Kingdom and Syria. However,
judgment was still to come their way. They had
also rebelled against the Lord and worshipped
other gods and had oppressed their own people.
As a result, the Lord promised swift destruction
for all of them. In Isaiah 10, God describes
Himself as a lumberjack chopping down a forest,
and that forest happened to be the nation of
Judah. *"Behold, the Lord GOD of hosts will lop the
boughs with terrifying power; the great in height will be
hewn down, and the lofty will be brought low. He will cut
down the thickets of the forest with an axe, and Lebanon
will fall by the Majestic One. (Isaiah 10:33-34)* Can you
imagine delivering such news to the nation of
Judah if you were Isaiah? What devastating words,
yet words that were well deserved for them.

Has God given up on Judah? Will He just
chop down the forest and set the place on fire with
no hope for the future? No, He has not given up

on His people. Chapter 11 begins with much promise. God continued the forest metaphor when He says, *"There shall come forth a shoot from the stump of Jesse, and a branch from his roots shall bear fruit." (Isaiah 11:1)* The forest is envisioned now as a huge mass of stumps with every tall tree felled. But one of those stumps holds the promise for the future. It was through this stump that a "shoot" comes up. A shoot from a fallen tree can only mean one thing — life! The "shoot" that comes from the stump continues to grow, and the tree becomes healthy again. It is now recognizable as a branch. A branch that is full of fruit and vitality. A branch that bears fruit is a sign of health and success.

Isaiah says that this stump is the family of Jesse. Jesse is the father of King David. The line of King David is the one from which the Messiah had been promised to come. The message was clear to Judah through Isaiah's words. Dark days were on the horizon — swift destruction was coming their way. Yet even after the forest had been chopped down and all appears to be dead, there is life! God was telling His people that even though they had forgotten Him and broken His covenant, He had not forgotten them and would keep His covenant with them. He would still send the Messiah in spite of their sin and rebellion. God is faithful.

Destruction did come to Judah some years later as Babylon and King Nebuchadnezzar were the instruments God used to destroy them. Jerusalem was rebuilt, and a "stump" from Jesse's family sprouted up with life. The Messianic line continued until "the Branch" was incarnated in Bethlehem. It is no coincidence either that Jesus grew up in Nazareth. He was called "Jesus the Nazarene." The word Nazareth comes from the word branch. Jesus is the branch that sprouted from Jesse's stump. He bears much fruit as He accomplishes His Father's will to redeem His people. Jesus is the Branch from Jesse's stump that bears fruit.

This is the One. Merry Christmas!

December 6th

The One Who Is Perfectly Patient

*The saying is trustworthy and deserving of full acceptance,
that Christ Jesus came into the world to save sinners, of
whom I am the foremost. But I received mercy for this
reason, that in me, as the foremost, Jesus Christ might
display his perfect patience as an example to those who were
to believe in him for eternal life.*
1 Timothy 1:15-16

Have you ever been with someone who
required a little extra patience when you were with
them? If you can't think of that one person, then
it's most likely that you are one of those people for
whom other people need patience. I'm joking of
course… or, am I? In this passage, Paul reflected
on God's "perfect patience" directed towards him.
Paul was the ideal candidate for God's immediate
judgment. However, Jesus is perfectly patient with
people just like Paul, which also includes all of us.
It is the very reason why He came.

Paul (also known as Saul) was indeed a person
who hated Jesus prior to his conversion. He had
some Christians imprisoned and even killed for
their faith. Paul's testimony is that, *"I persecuted this
Way to the death, binding and delivering to prison both*

men and women, as the high priest and the whole council of elders can bear me witness. From them I received letters to the brothers, and I journeyed toward Damascus to take those also who were there and bring them in bonds to Jerusalem to be punished." (Acts 22:4-5) It is no wonder that Paul thought of himself as the foremost of sinners. However, Jesus came into the world to save people just like Paul.

There should be no confusion as to why He came, but unfortunately there is still much confusion. Some believe the reason for Jesus' coming was for social reasons. They say He came to show us how to love, feed the poor, and care for the sick. There isn't a single verse in the Bible that says that Jesus came just for these specific reasons. Then what is *THE* reason for His coming?

Paul gives the answer in his first epistle to Timothy. Paul wrote, *"Christ Jesus came into the world to save sinners."* He came to save sinners! Paul said that this *"saying is trustworthy and deserving of full acceptance."* Paul knew that he needed a Savior. To paraphrase Paul, "Jesus came to save people like me! If you want proof of what kind of sinner Jesus came into the world for, look no further than me — I am the worst of sinners."

Paul reflected upon this "perfect patience" of Jesus although Paul was a wicked man and deserving of judgment.

God sent Jesus to people who hated Him. God loved us while we were still in love with our sin. (Romans 5:8) God chose us before we chose Him. (Ephesians 1:4-5) All of this was of God's doing and His Sovereign Grace. This was motivated by the desire to glorify Himself by exercising perfect patience with us. Paul writes saying that through Jesus is how God has patience with us, *"whom God put forward as a propitiation by his blood, to be received by faith. This was to show God's righteousness, because in his divine forbearance he had passed over former sins. It was to show his righteousness at the present time, so that he might be just and the justifier of the one who has faith in Jesus."* (Romans 3:24-25)

Some of us became Christians when we were quite young. Others of us became Christians later in life. No matter when we came to faith in Christ, God had to exhibit perfect patience with us. That baby in the manger, the One we are thinking about this month, He is evidence that God is patient with us.

This is the One. Merry Christmas!

December 7th

The One Who Is the Word

In the beginning was the Word, and the Word was with God, and the Word was God. — John 1:1

When we speak, we communicate who we are by our words. Our voices have a certain tone and others are able to recognize us by how we sound. We have accents (whether we know it or not) that are influenced often by where we live or who we live with. We may even have a certain way of saying things that display to others our character. In short, the words we speak and how we speak them are important in creating our identity. We can say that words are important. Words are a gift from God.

God Himself uses words. It was by His words that He created the universe. The first words spoken in the Bible were *"Let there be light."* (Genesis 1:1) God alone has the power and authority to speak things into existence. The Psalmist said, *"By the word of the Lord the heavens were made, and by the breath of his mouth all their host...For he spoke, and it came to be; he commanded, and it stood firm." (Psalm 33:6,9)* The words of the Lord are powerful words.

God also communicates to us through His word. The prophets of the Old Testament bellowed out, *"Thus says the Lord,"* when they gave the people the message that God intended for them to hear. It is God's word that warns, guides, rebukes, encourages, and saves us. Through actual words God makes Himself known. Today we are blessed to have God's word written down for us in the Bible. The Bible is God's written word. It is safe to say that without words we would not know what we know about God.

These truths are all the more amazing when you consider how John began his gospel. He describes a person who is known as "the Word." We know from the context of the chapter that John is speaking about Jesus. When you consider why John called Him "the Word," you will understand why Jesus is so important. If Jesus is the Word of God personified in human flesh, then to see and hear Jesus was to know and hear God. It is through Jesus that God the Father has made Himself known. Jesus said such remarkable things such as, *"Whoever has seen me has seen the Father."* *(John 14:9)* Jesus also said that to hear Him was to hear the Father, for He speaks the Father's words. (John 12:48-50) In addition, He said, *"If you knew me, you would know the Father also." (John 8:19)*

Jesus is God. He is also the full expression of God the Father and everything that can be known about the Father can be seen and heard from Him. As our spoken words help others know who we are, so Jesus "The Word" makes God the Father known to us. John wrote, *"No one has ever seen God; the only God, who is at the Father's side, he has made him known."* The writer of the book of Hebrews clarifies to us as well, *"Long ago, at many times and in many ways, God spoke to our fathers by the prophets, but in these last days he has spoken to us by his Son… (Hebrews 1:1-2)*

Christmas is the story of God making Himself known to the world by a Word. This Word is Jesus. Without Him we cannot know who God is, what He does, or how to please Him. Jesus is the Word who became flesh. He is the Word of God.

This is the One. Merry Christmas!

December 8th

The One Who Created

All things were made through him, and without him was not any thing made that was made. — John 1:3

It seems totally incomprehensible that the One who made the materials for the manger was laid to sleep in it as a newborn. That the One who created the womb of His mother was in that same womb for nine months. That the One who created the angels sent the same angels to announce His birth. That the One who created every star in the sky created the star to guide the wise men to Him. That the One who created gold, frankincense, and myrrh had those same things given to Him at His birth. That the same One who hung on a cross made the wood from which the cross was made. These are the thoughts that should cause us great pause this Christmas. It should humble us to see Christ as both the promise giver and the promise keeper. He is the Sovereign God who creates.

John tells us in the first verse of his gospel that the One who is also called the Word, was not only in the beginning with God, but was also Himself God. He was not a spectator on the heavenly sidelines. He created all things — all things! There was nothing made that wasn't made by Him. He made the sun, moon, and every star in the sky. He made mountains, oceans, rivers, and every animal and creature on earth. It is astounding to think of these things when you just think of Jesus as an infant in a manger. He was an infant in a manger, but He was also much more. Paul says, *"For by him all things were created, in heaven and on earth, visible and invisible, whether thrones or dominions or rulers or authorities-all things were created through him and for him. (Colossians 1:16)* Hebrews 1:2 also confirms this truth by telling us that it was through Jesus that the Father *"created the world."*

When we think of a baby, we think of the start of a new life. When Jesus was born in Bethlehem, it was not the beginning for Him. In fact, Jesus has no beginning. He is the eternal God of the universe who always has been and will always be. Jesus existed before He was in Mary's womb and this is hard for us to comprehend. Although He was born a newborn baby, He is older than the universe itself.

It is a humbling thought to think that the Creator came to us. Yes, this is a miracle, but it is nothing short of the grace of God on display. "*You know the grace of our Lord Jesus Christ, that though he was rich, yet for your sakes he became poor, so that you through his poverty might become rich." (2 Corinthians 8:9)*

J.I. Packer says that this is the true essence of Christmas. He says, "the taking of manhood by the Son is set before us in a way which shows us how we should ever view it—not simply as a marvel of nature, but rather as a wonder of grace."[3] This is our Creator! The One who created all things entered His own creation as a baby. This was an incredible moment of grace that should leave us in awe.

Let's stop to consider the marvels of Christmas. The Author who has been writing the history of the world wrote Himself into the story. Everything belongs to Him for it all comes from Him. Jesus is God. Jesus is the Creator.

This is the One. Merry Christmas!

---

[3] J.I Packer. *Knowing God.* Downers Grove, IL: InterVarsity Press, 1973, pg 59

December 9th

The One Who is Light

In him was life, and the life was the light of men. The light shines in the darkness, and the darkness has not overcome it. — John 1:4-5

I will confess that I love to decorate for Christmas. My family usually decorates for Christmas on the second Saturday of November each year. I know for some of you that is extremely early. However, we like to enjoy the decorations for as long as possible. (Yes, we even love to have the decorations up during Thanksgiving dinner.)

Christmas decorations make a place cheery and bright. I especially like Christmas lights. We have Christmas lights that hang outside, inside, and on our tree. The more lights the better! But what is the purpose of Christmas lights? How did that all begin? Legend has it that it was the 16th century reformer, Martin Luther, who popularized the tradition of the Christmas tree. Although there is no historical basis, legend says that Luther decided that it would be a good idea to put candles on trees to remember Christ at Christmas time.[4] I wonder what Martin Luther would think of our electric lights today? Why would lights on a tree be a reminder of Christ?

John referred to Jesus' being the "light" in the beginning of the gospel of John. It was something that John had heard from Jesus' own teaching. Jesus said, *"I am the light of the world. Whoever follows me will not walk in darkness, but will have the light of life." (John 8:12)* Jesus is the light of the world, for being God, He alone is holy. When Jesus was born in Bethlehem, He entered a sin-filled dark world that hated God. It was still the sin that Adam had introduced to creation in Genesis 3. This sin had caused a great darkness in the hearts of men and had alienated them from God. He is the light that breaks through the darkness to expose sin for what it is, a robber of God's glory.

John also said that the darkness cannot overcome this light. Isn't that the nature of light? The only way the darkness can win is if the light goes away. Darkness does not make a room less bright. It is only when the source of the light leaves that darkness enters. John was telling his

---

[4]https://www.christianitytoday.com/history/2008/december/why-do-we-have-christmas-trees.html

readers that once Jesus was born, the light was here and would always be here.

How did Jesus defeat the darkness? He defeated the darkness by overcoming sin in obedience to God's law. He removed the curse *from* us by becoming a curse *for* us — by hanging on a tree. The New Testament writers sometimes referred to the cross as the "tree." This is what Paul told the Galatians, *"Christ redeemed us from the curse of the law by becoming a curse for us-for it is written, "Cursed is everyone who is hanged on a tree."*
(Galatians 3:13)

Peter also wrote, *"He himself bore our sins in his body on the tree, that we might die to sin and live to righteousness. By his wounds you have been healed."*
(1 Peter 2:24)

This Christmas season, when you admire the beauty of your Christmas tree and see the lights on that tree, may you reflect on the Light of the World who was crucified on a tree. It is He whose light is so glorious that it defeats the darkness of sin, death, hell, and the power of the evil one. We need light. We live in darkness with dark hearts. We need Jesus.

This is the One. Merry Christmas!

December 10th

The One Who Became Flesh

And the Word became flesh and dwelt among us...
John 1:14

The grace of God was not just that God wrote Himself into the story but that He *"dwelt among us."* God didn't just become a man, He lived among men as a man. Why did Jesus have to live on earth? If Jesus' mission was to *"seek and save the lost"* *(Luke 19:10)* then why did He come into the world as a baby? Why live thirty-three years on earth? Why not just fast-forward the plan and die on a cross and rise again from the dead? Wouldn't that have fulfilled God's plan? No, it would not have.

God's plan was for Jesus to become a man and live among sinners. Jesus didn't just come to pay the penalty of sin; He came to fulfill the law of God. Jesus came to complete the law because we were unable to keep it ourselves. Jesus said, *"Do not think that I have come to abolish the Law or the Prophets; I have not come to abolish them but to fulfill them." (Matthew 5:17)*

Eugene Peterson paraphrased John 1:14 this way, *"And the Word became flesh and blood and moved into the neighborhood."*[5] What does it mean that, *"he moved into the neighborhood?"* Well, a neighborhood is a personal thing. Your neighborhood is where your home is located. Your neighborhood is a part of you and is familiar. Jesus didn't come for a quick visit like family at Thanksgiving. He actually decided to live here among us. He didn't send a representative but came Himself. He breathed the same air and walked on the same dirt. He came to where we lived. He experienced our joy and our pain.

In Jesus, we see that God is not distant. The Greek word for "dwelt" is the same word that means "to pitch a tent." It also means to live, to settle, or to reside.[6] Jesus didn't come in Spirit but in flesh and blood. He came and lived on earth. God has always chosen to be close to His people. In the wilderness journey His Spirit came and filled the tabernacle. This time, however, would be different. God would not just come in the Spirit but in human flesh and blood. God chose to be born, grow up, and become a man. The Holy God

---

[5] Eugene H. Peterson. *The Message: The Bible in Contemporary Language.* Colorado Springs: NavPress, 2002

[6] Barry, John D. et al. *Faithlife Study Bible* (Bellingham, WA: Logos Bible Software, 2012) John 1:14

of the universe came to our neighborhood. This gives us the confidence that He does actually care and love us.

J.I. Packer writes, "The Word had become flesh: a real human baby. He had not ceased to be God; he was no less God then than before; but he had begun to be man. He was not now God *minus* some elements of his deity, but God plus all that he had made his own by taking manhood to himself."[7]

He could have stayed far away. He could have watched us kill ourselves with our own sin. He didn't. God came knocking on the doors of our neighborhood and took up residence. When your heart grows weary, reflect on this truth. God is not distant, and Jesus is proof. He moved into our neighborhood. Man had separated Himself from God by his sin; God has now come to us through the incarnation of Jesus. Christmas is not just about a random young couple who gave birth to a baby in a manger. It is God's announcement that I am here with you, and this is good news.

This is the One. Merry Christmas!

---

[7] J.I Packer. *Knowing God.*, pg 59

December 11th

The One Who Has Glory

And the Word became flesh and dwelt among us, and
we have seen his glory, glory as of the only Son from the
Father, full of grace and truth. — John 1:14

John knew that Jesus was different for he beheld Him with his own eyes. The shepherds knew that Jesus was different as told to them by the angels. The wisemen also knew that Jesus was different for they journeyed from afar to see Him for themselves. John says that *"we have seen his glory."* The glory that John speaks of here is not of celebrity fame. Sometimes people are often starstruck at the sight of a famous person. Jesus was not glorious because He was well-known in His day. He was glorious for a totally different reason. John says that His glory is one that is *"of the only Son from the Father, full of grace and truth."* Jesus shares the same glory as God the Father. That is something that not a single person or creature in creation can claim.

As image bearers of God, we reflect the glory of God. However, in Jesus, we don't see a reflection of glory; we see actual glory. This is what the writer of Hebrews says, *"He is the radiance of the glory of God and the exact imprint of his nature, and he upholds the universe by the word of his power." (Hebrews 1:3)* Nothing else in the universe possesses this inherent glory. This is what it means when the writer says that, *"He is the radiance of the glory of God."* Jesus can do so because He is the *"exact imprint of His nature."*

We must behold the glory of Christ. The word glory in the Bible often speaks of the worth and value of God. God is worthy of our worship for He is glorious. He is glorious for He is holy. There is nothing wrong with enjoying things in this life. However, when we attribute the glory to them that is solely reserved for God and God alone, we sin. It is seeing the glory of Christ that will help us overcome sin and resist temptation. What is more glorious to you, Jesus or your sin? It is seeing God as glorious that will enable us to withstand any and all trials in this world.

Have you ever wondered why the disciples changed so rapidly after the crucifixion? They saw the glory of the resurrected Christ; a glory so bright and beautiful, that on the road to Damascus it opened the heart of a wicked man named Saul (Acts 9). It is the glory of Christ that we need this Christmas. We don't need fancy toys or sentimental gifts. Those are nice, but are not what we need. We need to see that Jesus is glorious.

One of the most familiar Christmas hymns is "Gloria in Excelsis Deo." This is a Latin phrase that means "Glory to God in the highest." This is, in fact, exactly what the angels proclaimed to the shepherds. *"Glory to God in the highest, and on earth peace among those with whom he is pleased!" (Luke 2:14)* What a fitting thing to say as the King of Glory was born in Bethlehem. Jesus should be more glorious to us than any Christmas tradition we can observe annually. Jesus should be more glorious to us than anything we can receive as a gift.

How do you see the glory of Christ this Christmas? How weighty is He to your family? What holds more worth than Him in your life? Jesus is glorious. Jesus is the glory of God. Anything else that replaces or attempts to substitute this glory is idolatry. Jesus is the glory we must behold from God.

This is the One. Merry Christmas!

December 12th

The One Who Came in the Fullness of Time

But when the fullness of time had come, God sent forth his Son, born of woman, born under the law, to redeem those who were under the law, so that we might receive adoption as sons. - Galatians 4:4-5

When I was a child, it felt as if Christmas was never going to arrive. The days dragged on as I anticipated opening my Christmas gifts. I often begged my mother and negotiated with her about opening up gifts early, but I never won. Can you believe even my wife refuses to let me open gifts early? Yes, I know I'm still a kid at heart and just love Christmas, but now that I'm an adult, Christmas doesn't seem to take as long to arrive. It's amazing how time flies when you are the main one responsible for buying presents for others.

I can imagine that this is how some Jews felt about the Messiah. God had promised through the prophets, as early as the third chapter of Genesis, that a Messiah would come. A long time had passed since that initial promise was made, yet there was still no Messiah. A man named Simeon felt that way as he greatly anticipated the arrival of the Messiah. Luke tells us, *"Now there was a man in*

*Jerusalem, whose name was Simeon, and this man was
righteous and devout, waiting for the consolation of Israel,
and the Holy Spirit was upon him. And it had been
revealed to him by the Holy Spirit that he would not see
death before he had seen the Lord's Christ. (Luke 2:25-
26)*

The Holy Spirit told Simeon that he would not
die without seeing the Messiah. What a promise to
be given to this man. Simeon, your wait is about to
be over. You will see what you've been expecting
all of your life. I can just imagine the anticipation
as he awoke each morning. "Is today the day?
How much longer, Lord?"

One day his waiting ended, as Mary and Joseph
walked into the temple eight days after Jesus' birth
to dedicate Him according to the law. Simeon cast
his eyes on Jesus and said, *"Lord, now you are letting
your servant depart in peace, according to your word; for my
eyes have seen your salvation that you have prepared in the
presence of all peoples, a light for revelation to the Gentiles,
and for glory to your people Israel." (Luke 2:29-32)*
Simeon had received the best gift imaginable. He
had witnessed with his own eyes what the Lord
had been promising for thousands of years. The
wait had been worth it.

It was the perfect time that God had ordained to send His Son. Oh, and what a perfect time it was indeed. Thomas Watson once wrote, "He was born of a virgin, that we might be born of God. He took our flesh, that He might give us His Spirit. He lay in the manger that we might lie in paradise. He came down from heaven, that He might bring us to heaven. And what was all this but love? If our hearts be not rocks, this love of Christ should affect us. Behold love that surpasses knowledge (Ephesians 3:19)!"[8]

Paul told the Galatians that Jesus had come in the "fullness of time." God did not delay nor forget His promise of a Messiah. He had planned for just the right moment in time to send His Son. For a child, Christmas is all about the waiting—the expectation, the excitement. May we not lose that fervor as adults. May we anticipate Christmas with joyful, expectant, and worshipful hearts. May we worship God knowing that our salvation has come, and His name is Jesus, and He is worth the wait. Jesus is the One we anticipate.

This is the One. Merry Christmas!

---

[8] Thomas Watson. *A Body of Divinity*. Monergism Books: 2015, pg 374

December 13th

The One Who Came from the Spirit

But as he considered these things, behold, an angel of the Lord appeared to him in a dream, saying, "Joseph, son of David, do not fear to take Mary as your wife, for that which is conceived in her is from the Holy Spirit.
Matthew 1:20

Joseph was considering the possibility that Mary had been unfaithful during their betrothal. This news, if true, would be heartbreaking. However, the Lord sent an angel to give Joseph some good news in a dream that night. The news was good but almost inconceivable. Mary had not been unfaithful, but she had miraculously conceived a child from the Holy Spirit. Mary had not known another man, and indeed she was still a virgin.

Why is it significant for Matthew to tell us that Mary had conceived a child from the Holy Spirit? For one, it would be important for the Messiah to be born of a virgin. If Mary had known another man, she could not have been the mother of the Messiah. Matthew was establishing the fact that Jesus was indeed born of a virgin. We'll talk about this more in just a few days.

In addition, the Messiah would be one who would have the Holy Spirit with Him His entire life. Jesus came from the Holy Spirit, grew up with the Holy Spirit, ministered in the power of the Holy Spirit, and then sent the Holy Spirit to be with His people until He returned. The Messiah was to be One who was full of the presence and power of the Holy Spirit.

Isaiah prophesied in 11:2 that, *"the Spirit of the LORD shall rest upon him, the Spirit of wisdom and understanding, the Spirit of counsel and might, the Spirit of knowledge and the fear of the LORD. - (Isaiah 11:2)* The Messiah would also be anointed by the Spirit. *"The Spirit of the Lord GOD is upon me, because the LORD has anointed me to bring good news to the poor; he has sent me to bind up the brokenhearted, to proclaim liberty to the captives, and the opening of the prison to those who are bound; (Isaiah 61:1)* This is a passage that Jesus read in the synagogue and declared that it was about Him. (See Luke 4:18-22)

The Spirit was present at Jesus' baptism (Matthew 3:16), and before, during, and after His temptation (Luke 4:1,14). Jesus did miracles in the power of the Spirit (Matthew 12:18, Acts 10:38), offered Himself through death by the Spirit

(Hebrews 9:14), and was resurrected by the power of the Holy Spirit (Romans 8:11).

The Holy Spirit was extremely important in the life and ministry of Jesus. If Jesus were so dependent on the Spirit for every aspect of His life. Then why should we be any different?

May we realize today that the fact that the Holy Spirit was upon Jesus is proof that He's the Messiah. (1 Timothy 3:16) May we also know that without the Spirit there is no Christmas. Jesus comes from the Holy Spirit.

This is the One. Merry Christmas!

December 14th

The One Who Saves His People

She will bear a son, and you shall call his name Jesus,
for he will save his people from their sins."
Matthew 1:21

Deciding on what to name a baby could prove to be a challenging task for new parents. However, Joseph and Mary had no trouble whatsoever. The angel, who had told Joseph the good news about the baby's being from the Holy Spirit, now instructed Joseph what to name Him. This name came from God who had sent the angel to Joseph in a dream. The name of the baby was to be Jesus. The angel even gave a reason for naming the baby with this name, *"for he will save his people from their sins."* The name Jesus means "the Lord saves." There could be no more appropriate name for Him.

Jesus' name captures both His identity and His mission. The Lord saves. The prophet Joel prophesied, *"And it shall come to pass that everyone who calls on the name of the LORD shall be saved."(Joel 2:32)* It is this prophecy that Peter and Paul quote as they share the promise of the gospel. Peter stood up on the day of Pentecost and said it (Acts

2:21), and Paul also used it famously in Romans 10:13. It is a biblical way to describe those who have come to know God by His grace through faith. (1 Timothy 1:15)

However, the question becomes why does His people need to be saved? The word "saved" also means "delivered," so a Christian is a person who has been delivered from something or someone. This begs the question, "from what or whom has the Christian been delivered?" For these answers we must look to the Scriptures.

Jesus was born to save His people *"from their sins."* Here is our first clue in what we are delivered from, our sins. Sin is the breaking of God's law (1 John 3:4) which is a revelation of His character and nature. God is holy, righteous, and good. Sin is the violation of God's order and a thief of His glory. God is the exact opposite of sin in every way imaginable. Sin is the reason that the world is cursed (Genesis 3:17, Isaiah 24:6); man is separated from God (Isaiah 59:2) and stands in judgment (1 Peter 4:5, Revelation 20:11-13). Sin is the reason that there is death (Romans 6:23), disease, and decay. Sin corrupts the image of God that is inherent within each human being.

Many times, when Christians refer to being "saved," they think of where they will or will not spend eternity. Yes, it is true that a Christian is someone who will not go to hell or the lake of fire (Revelation 20:15). However, there is a much deeper reality to this that must be considered. God not only saves us from a place, but He also saves us from His wrath. (Romans 5:9) Let us not forget that God is not only the Savior, but He is also the Judge (Romans 2:16). Because we are sinners, we stand guilty in the presence of God. We are law breakers who deserve whatever sentence the law says must be given. (Ezekiel 18:20)

May you realize this Christmas that Jesus wasn't born so that we would have nice gifts and sentimental feelings about a holiday. As C.S. Lewis puts it, "The Son of God became a man to enable men to become sons of God."[9]

I understand that there might be some reading this book who don't know Christ in a saving way. My prayer is that they will repent of their sins and trust in Christ for salvation. This is exactly who Jesus is and why He has come.

Jesus was born to save.

This is the One. Merry Christmas!

---

[9] C.S Lewis. *Mere Christianity.* (HarperCollins Publishers, New York, 1952) pg. 178

December 15th

The One Who is God With Us

*All this took place to fulfill what the Lord had spoken
by the prophet: "Behold, the virgin shall conceive and bear a
son, and they shall call his name Immanuel" (which means,
God with us). — Matthew 1:22-23*

Matthew knew exactly what the birth of Jesus
fulfilled. He draws our attention back to the
prophet Isaiah who prophesied about the
Messiah's birth. Isaiah said that the sign the Lord
would give would be a virgin conceiving a child.
That is indeed a miraculous sign and could not be
mistaken as being anything except from the Lord.
We have already established that the Holy Spirit
came upon Mary and conceived Jesus in her
womb. (Luke 1:35) Jesus, therefore, did not have a
biological earthly father. He is unlike any other
baby born in history. Did the Lord do that just so
that we could marvel at the wonder of this
immaculate conception? No, He did not. There is
a vastly important doctrinal truth behind the virgin
birth.

If Jesus were to have an earthly father, He
would have inherited the guilt and wages of sin
from Adam. (See Romans 5:12) This would have
made Jesus a sinner (like us) and therefore He

could not have been the Savior that we needed. Instead, Jesus had God as His Father (as it was in Heaven) and therefore He was born with a divine nature that was given when the Holy Spirit entered Mary's womb. If Jesus were not born of a virgin, then our Christian faith would be in vain. The doctrine of the virgin birth of Christ is one of the most foundational doctrines of the faith.

Jesus was the God-man. He was God incarnated into human flesh. God did not send an angel or another representative from heaven. God came Himself to earth to fulfill all of His promises. Isaiah's prophecy said that the name of this virgin born son would be Immanuel. Immanuel is a title that represents who this baby was to be. Matthew helps us out with the interpretation of the name and says that it means "God with us."

Laying in the manger that night was not just a baby; the baby was God. When Mary held Him and kissed Him, she was kissing the face of God. This was an amazing moment in history. Never before has anyone ever seen the face of God. However, now, Mary could look into her baby's eyes and kiss His cheeks. The Jewish people knew that to see God was a death sentence. Moses had made a request to God so that he could see God's glory. God had told Moses that if He were to grant his request that he would die. (See Exodus 33:20)

So, therefore, no one has ever stood in God's presence and seen God. All of that changes with Jesus. John confirms this for us by saying, *"No one has ever seen God; the only God, who is at the Father's side, He has made him known." (John 1:18)* Now people could not only stand in God's presence and live, but also touch Him and see His face. He is God with us.

Jesus has made known God the Father to us. When Jesus walked with people on earth; they walked with God. When they heard Him speak; they heard God speak. When they sat down to eat a meal; they ate a meal with God. What a gift. What a blessing. This is something Moses could only have dreamed of doing in His day. However, now that the Messiah has come, Jesus has made what was impossible for Moses possible for the world.

This is one of the great treasures of Christmas. This was not just good news for those who lived in Jesus' day. This is good news for all who love Him and are one of His own. This will be our reality for eternity. We will be with our God and He will be with us. It's an encouragement not just for tomorrow but also for today. (1 John 3:2, Revelation 21:1-27)

This is the One. Merry Christmas!

December 16th

The One Who Is Worshipped

When they saw the star, they rejoiced exceedingly with great joy. And going into the house, they saw the child with Mary his mother, and they fell down and worshiped him. Then, opening their treasures, they offered him gifts, gold and frankincense and myrrh. - Matthew 2:10-11

The wise men made their way to see Jesus after seeing the star in the sky. They knew what it meant and came with expectations of worshipping Him. They explained to Herod, *"Where is he who has been born king of the Jews? For we saw his star when it rose and have come to worship him." (Matthew 2:2)* Herod inquired of the religious leaders about the Messianic prophecies and learned that Bethlehem was to be the birthplace. As a result, he sent the wise men to Bethlehem to search for Jesus. Herod had no intentions of worshipping Jesus but had his own wicked plans. The wise men made their way to Bethlehem and the star they had seen at the beginning of the journey reappeared and led them to where Jesus was staying.

They were full of joy when they saw the star. As they made their way into the house and saw Him and Mary, they fell down and worshipped

Him. They brought Him gifts of gold, frankincense and myrrh. They were worshipping Christ.

This is what we often miss about Christmas. Christmas is a wonderful time to be with family, have sweet traditions that are passed on to future generations, and to relax after a busy year. As wonderful as sentimentalities, traditions, and family are during the "most wonderful time of the year," they are no match for worshipping Christ. If you are doing Christmas without worship, you are doing it wrong. Pause and reflect, read, listen, give thanks, and celebrate Jesus with your family.

It was not just the wise men who worshipped Jesus in the Christmas narrative. The angels worshipped as they delivered the news to the shepherds! *"And suddenly there was with the angel a multitude of the heavenly host praising God and saying, "Glory to God in the highest, and on earth peace among those with whom he is pleased!" (Luke 2:13-14)*

The shepherds worshipped! *"And the shepherds returned, glorifying and praising God for all they had heard and seen, as it had been told them." (Luke 2:20)*

Mary worshipped! *"But Mary treasured up all these things, pondering them in her heart. (Luke 2:19)*

Eight days later, Simeon worshipped! *"And he came in the Spirit into the temple, and when the parents brought in the child Jesus, to do for him according to the custom of the Law, he took him up in his arms and blessed God…" (Luke 2:27-28)*

Anna the prophetess worshipped! *"And coming up at that very hour she began to give thanks to God and to speak of him to all who were waiting for the redemption of Jerusalem. (Luke 2:38)*

What is your family doing to worship Christ this Christmas? I am not referring to attending Christmas Eve services at your church. What is your family doing to treasure Christ as the wise men did? I pray that these devotionals thus far have provided a spark for you to worship with your family. Jesus is worthy of our worship not just for today, but forevermore.

This is the One. Merry Christmas!

December 17th

The One Whose Kingdom Has No End

He will be great and will be called the Son of the Most
High. And the Lord God will give to him the throne of his
father David, and he will reign over the house of Jacob
forever, and of his kingdom there will be no end."
Luke 1:32-33

The words of the Hallelujah Chorus from
Handel's Messiah are repetitive, but they are
majestic. The song has become a classic part of the
Christmas season that delivers the meaning of
Christmas. Jesus is the Son of the Most High! He
is the omnipotent God of creation. He is the
Almighty God who reigns over all. Here are some
of the main lyrics from Handel's classic.
"Hallelujah! For the Lord God omnipotent
reigneth… King of kings (for ever and
ever)…And Lord of lords (hallelujah,
hallelujah)…And He shall reign for ever and ever."

These majestic words are what the angel told
Mary about her soon to be born baby boy. Mary
would be the virgin who was chosen to give birth
to the Messiah. Mary's baby would be the One to
sit on the throne of David. There had not been a
real king to sit on this throne of David since the

destruction of Judah in 586 BC. The nation of Judah had become wicked, forsaking God and His law, and had gone after idols. As a result, God destroyed them with the armies of Babylon led by Nebuchadnezzar. This left the throne of David empty and it appeared that God had forgotten His promise. However, God had not forgotten His promise and would keep His promises.

Long before the judgment fell on Judah, God had made a promise to David through the prophet Nathan. (See 2 Samuel 7:10, 1 Chronicles 17:11-14). Solomon, who was the next king of Israel, and also the son of David, prayed to God saying, *"Now therefore, O Lord, God of Israel, keep for your servant David my father what you have promised him, saying, 'You shall not lack a man to sit before me on the throne of Israel, if only your sons pay close attention to their way, to walk in my law as you have walked before me.'"*

Israel had no king on the throne then and still has no king on the throne now. However, God's promise is certain that the Messiah would sit on David's throne once again. The kings of Judah (see 1st and 2nd Samuel, 1st and 2nd Kings, 1st and 2nd Chronicles) all reigned and died. Some of them reigned for a short time while others reigned for a long time. However, none of them were the fulfillment to God's covenant with David.

What the angel told Mary changed everything. The angel did not just say that there would be a king on David's throne once again. He said that Jesus would sit on that throne forever! There will be no end to His reign as King. When a king's reign ends, it usually means that the king has died and/or has been defeated in battle by the enemy. Jesus reigning forever on the throne means that He will never die again and that He will never be defeated by the enemy. What joyous news for Mary to hear, and not just Mary but all who trust in Him. Jesus is King.

John addressed the letter of Revelation to seven churches. Listen to how confident John is in the Kingdom of Christ. *"Jesus Christ the faithful witness, the firstborn of the dead, and the ruler of kings on earth. To him who loves us and has freed us from our sins by his blood and made us a kingdom, priests to his God and Father, to him be glory and dominion forever and ever. Amen. (Revelation 1:5-6)*

This is the One. Merry Christmas!

December 18th

The One Who Is "Holy - the Son of God"

...therefore the child to be born will be called holy - the Son of God. — Luke 1:35

The angel had already revealed to Mary some remarkable news about her baby. However, the glorious news about Him never ends. The angel told Mary that the baby would be *"holy - the Son of God."* Jesus comes *"from the Holy Spirit"* so logically it would make sense that He is also holy. However, He is not just holy because of the Holy Spirit. He was already holy before He was born. As we have already discussed, Jesus is the Pre-existent One. His existence predates Bethlehem and time itself. The word "holy" signifies to us that He is without sin; He is pure and righteous. The word "holy" also has a connotation of separation and uniqueness. Jesus is different from the rest of creation because He possesses inherent holiness.

I think most mothers would say that their newborn baby is special. However, for Mary, her baby was more than special. He was *"holy — the Son of God."* The title Son of God is used to establish Jesus' divinity. He is not God's Son in the sense that He was created (more on that later) but in the sense that He bears the same attributes and divine essence of God the Father. It is a title that describes His nature. A similar observation can be made when we see that Jesus nicknames John and James the *"sons of thunder."* (Mark 3:17) Jesus wasn't saying that James and John literally were sons of a man/god named thunder. However, their personality, charisma, and actions resembled thunder. They were probably loud and boisterous like thunder. Likewise, when Jesus is called Son of God, it is in reference to His divine nature with God the Father.

We must not miss out this Christmas on the fact that Jesus is holy. Many of us are familiar with Isaiah 6 in which Isaiah sees in a vision the Lord sitting on a throne. If you have never read that passage, please pause and read it now (Isaiah 6:1-8). In this passage, Isaiah hears the cherubim and seraphim repeatedly proclaim, *"Holy, holy, holy is the LORD of hosts; the whole earth is full of his glory!" (Isaiah 6:3)*

Fire, smoke, and the shaking of the very foundations of that worship service were moved with the praise of this Holy God. Wow, what a scene. God is Holy! God's holiness is what separates Him from you and me. The seraphim spoke the word "holy" three times. This is a declaration of the nature of God in Trinity.

Jesus is the second person of the Trinity. He is the Son of God. John provides further clarity as to what Isaiah saw in this vision. Isaiah says he saw *"the Lord."* John says, *"Isaiah said these things because he saw his glory and spoke of him. (John 12:41)* John clarifies for us that who John saw was indeed Jesus. Jesus is the holy Son of God. Jesus has inherent holiness.

This is the One. Merry Christmas!

December 19th

The One Who Was First Born

*And she gave birth to her firstborn son and wrapped
him in swaddling cloths and laid him in a manger, because
there was no place for them in the inn.*
Luke 2:7

Jesus was the firstborn son of Mary. Mary had
other children as recorded for us in the Bible.
(Mark 6:3, Matthew 13:55-56) Jesus, of course, was
her firstborn since Mary was a virgin. However,
there are other places where Jesus is listed as being
firstborn. The doctrine of "firstborn" is an
important doctrine to learn and study as we
consider the nature and identity of Christ.

Paul wrote to the Colossians, *"He is the image of
the invisible God, the firstborn of all creation." (Colossians
1:15)* When we think of the term "firstborn," we
normally think of the order of birth as in Luke 2:7.
Jesus was indeed the first born to Mary in a
biological sense, just as I am the first born in my
family. I have two younger siblings, a brother and
a sister. I was born first, so I am the first born. I
know that doesn't take rocket science to
understand. However, when Paul mentions that
Jesus is the *"firstborn of all creation,"* it does not mean

the same thing as biological order of birth. This does not mean that Jesus was the first being created in creation. That is an ancient heresy known as Arianism. Jesus is not a created being. He is the eternal God. If Jesus were created, that would mean He is not God. Remember, that John tells us in 1:1 that *"In the beginning was the Word, and the Word was with God, and the Word was God."*

If firstborn doesn't mean biological order of birth, then what does it mean? In Israel there was a special privilege granted to the firstborn. The firstborn was given the blessing of the family, a double inheritance, and took over the role of the head of the family. Therefore, the word firstborn, in this way, refers more to the status and authority of the person because of the position given. Jesus is the firstborn of creation in the sense that He is the most important of all of creation. Jesus said, *"All authority in heaven and on earth has been given to me." (Matthew 28:18)* This is speaking of His position of power and authority. God the Father has highly exalted Him and given Him a name above all names. (Philippians 2:9-11)

Paul also tells us, *"For those whom he foreknew he also predestined to be conformed to the image of his Son, in order that he might be the firstborn among many brothers. (Romans 8:29)* We who believe are being conformed into His image. He is the One through whom God is adopting a family. He is the most important One. Jesus is the mold through whom God is making a family unto Himself, and this family is holy.

Paul also tells us that, *"He is the head of the body, the church, as well as the beginning, the firstborn from among the dead so that he himself may become first in all things." (Colossians 1:18)* Here is another way to see this beautiful truth. Jesus is the most important person ever to die because He has conquered death and because He has been resurrected. There were other people in the Bible who were resurrected from the dead, but nobody was raised in their own power. Their resurrection did not alter history or change anything for anyone. However, through Jesus' resurrection, all those who believe in Him also live.

John Piper writes, "He is a big God for little people, and we have great cause to rejoice that, unbeknownst to them, all the kings and presidents and premiers and chancellors of the world follow the sovereign decrees of our Father in heaven, that we, the children, might be conformed to the image of His Son, Jesus Christ."[10]

Jesus is the firstborn. He was not just born first to Mary; He is the firstborn in life and death.

This is the One. Merry Christmas!

[10] John Piper. *Good News of Great Joy: Daily Readings for Advent.* (Desiring God, Minneapolis, 2013) pg 8

December 20th

The One Who Is Good News of Great Joy

*And the angel said to them, "Fear not, for behold, I
bring you good news of great joy that will be for all the
people. - Luke 2:10*

The first to have the news of the Messiah's
birth announced to them were shepherds. That
may not sound too surprising to you because you
are familiar with the story. However, I believe it
would not have been the way some would have
written it. Shepherds in Israel were considered to
be a lower class. They were often dirty and smelly
from caring for their flocks. Yet, God chose them,
of all the people, to hear the news that the world
had been waiting to hear. In a similar way, God did
the same thing with the news of the resurrection.
Who were the first to hear the news? It was
women who heard the news first. In those days, a
woman's testimony was not considered to be a
valid source of the truth and could not be used in a
court of law. However, it was the women who first
heard the news about the empty tomb. It was just
like the Lord to deliver the message in counter-
cultural ways.

This news according to the angel was *"for all the people."* Shepherds? Yes, even shepherds. How about the blind? The lame? Lepers? Political zealots? Tax Collectors? Fishermen? Is this just good news for Jews? What about Gentiles? The angels said that this was good news for all the people. Jesus didn't come just for the rich He also came for the poor. He didn't come just for men, but He also came for women. He didn't just come for Israel; He also came to be the Savior for the nations. We should be reminded today about the universal nature of the good news that is available to all men, women, and children around the world. Not all will receive this as good news, but if by faith they trust in Christ it will *be "good news of great joy."* Whether or not someone accepts this as good news does not change it from being good news. It is good news regardless.

The angel arrived with a glorious light and made the great pronouncement, *"Fear not, for behold, I bring you good news of great joy that will be for all the people." (Luke 2:10)* The shepherds must have been extremely frightened, for the first words the angel said were, "fear not." What the angels were essentially saying was, "This is not news that will bring judgment to you; do not fear." The news the angel gave was more than just good news. It was *"good news of great joy."* That's better than good news. It's news that will be water to your dry and thirsty soul. This news should produce in you a great joy.

It is good news of great joy because of what the incarnation represents. Piper writes, "The reason Jesus became man was to die. As God, he could not die for sinners. But as man he could. His aim was to die. Therefore, He had to be born human. He was born to die. Good Friday is the reason for Christmas. This is what needs to be said today about the meaning of Christmas."[11] Yes, believe it or not, Christmas and Good Friday are based on the same foundational truth.

What brings you joy today? Perhaps it's an anticipation of a certain gift you hope to receive in just a few short days. No matter how great that gift might be, it will only bring a temporary joy. However, the good news of great joy of Christmas is that Christ has come, and He has won.

Jesus is good news of great joy.

This is the One. Merry Christmas!

---

[11] John Piper. *Good News of Great Joy: Daily Readings for Advent.* pg 8

December 21st

The One Who Is the Greater Prophet

"The LORD your God will raise up for you a prophet like me from among you, from your brothers—it is to him you shall listen—just as you desired of the LORD your God at Horeb on the day of the assembly, when you said, 'Let me not hear again the voice of the LORD my God or see this great fire any more, lest I die.'"
Deuteronomy 18:15–16

There are three Old Testament offices that God gave the nation of Israel. One of them was the office of prophet. A prophet was someone who received a message from God and delivered it to the people. The prophet was a messenger of God. He received what God wanted to say to His people and then delivered it. The people were afraid to hear the voice of the Lord directly. Therefore, they needed someone to go before them for they feared they might die. *"For who is there of all flesh, that has heard the voice of the living God speaking out of the midst of fire as we have, and has still lived? Go near and hear all that the LORD our God will say, and speak to us all that the LORD our God will speak to you, and we will hear and do it."* (Deuteronomy 5:25–27)

Moses was that kind of prophet to Israel as he led them out of Egypt and into the wilderness. Moses was the divine representative Israel needed for that time.

However, Moses would not live forever. He was human and eventually died. After Moses died, the Lord raised other great prophets that ministered to His people — Joshua, Samuel, Nathan, Elijah, Isaiah, Micah, Nahum, Jeremiah, Ezekiel, Daniel, Haggai, etc. These men were also divine representatives. When they spoke, *"Thus says the Lord...,"* it was as if God was speaking through them. To obey the prophet's words (as long as they were God's words) was to obey God. To disobey the prophet's words was also to disobey God. None of these prophets lived forever. They all lived for a time and then they all died. Thankfully, God has preserved His word so that we can still know what the prophets said to the people. We hold those words of God today in our Bibles. Amazing!

Before Moses died, he made a prophetic promise. He told the Israelites in Deuteronomy 18:15-16 that God would raise them up another prophet just like him. Moses instructed the people to listen to this prophet just as they had listened to him. The prophet he spoke of was the Messiah. This was another Messianic prophecy to prepare the hearts of Israel. When John the Baptist was preaching, the religious leaders asked him if he was "the Prophet." This was in reference to the Mosaic prophecy of Deuteronomy 18. John said he was not *that* prophet. Later John tells us that the crowds attributed the fulfillment of Moses' prophecy to Jesus in John 6:14 saying, *"This is indeed the Prophet who is to come into the world!"*

As a prophet, the Messiah would speak the words of God. The Apostle Peter, on the Day of Pentecost, confirmed to us that Jesus is the fulfillment of Moses' prophecy. (See Acts 3:23-26) Jesus is indeed that Prophet! Jesus said that His words are not His own but *"him who sent me."* (John 7:16) He also said He speaks as the *"Father taught me." (John 8:28)* Jesus said He didn't speak on His own initiative but spoke as the Father had told Him to speak. (John 12:49-50). The Father also told us to listen to Him, *"This is my beloved Son, with whom I am well pleased; listen to him." (Matthew 17:5)* Jesus doesn't just speak the words of God as a normal prophet. He speaks as God. Jesus never had to say, *"Thus says the Lord,"* as the other prophets had done before. He was the Lord! So every word that came from His mouth was the Lord God speaking.

Jesus is the Prophet that was to come into the world. He is greater than Moses. He is the One through whom God has spoken and we should listen to Him.

This is the One. Merry Christmas!

December 22nd

The One Who Is the Greater High Priest

And being made perfect, he became the source of eternal salvation to all who obey him, being designated by God a high priest after the order of Melchizedek.
Hebrews 5:9-10

The second office of the Old Testament was that of priest. Yesterday we saw that the prophets represented God to the people. The priests were different from the prophets in that they represented man to God. They had the duty to pray, offer sacrifices, and ensure that all God required for worship was ready for the people. The office of priest was a gift of God to the people so they could have a mediation for their sin and ensure their relationship with God. The priests came from one specific tribe, the tribe of Levi.

There was one priest who was above the rest and had duties that none of the other priests could perform. This priest would enter the Holy of Holies in the tabernacle/temple, once a year, and make atonement for sins by sprinkling the blood of the sacrifice on the mercy seat of the Ark of the Covenant. Without the priests there could not be this yearly atonement, as the people needed someone to represent them to God.

This sacrificial system was instituted by God for a season because it could not be a permanent solution for the sins of the world. It served as a type of what was to come. God had not just promised the forgiveness of sins for the Jewish people, but for Gentiles (all other ethnicities) as well. God had commanded that Israel, through the High Priest, on one day of the year make a special atonement for sins. This special day is called Yom Kippur (Day of Atonement). Yom Kippur was never intended to be a permanent solution for the sins of God's people. It was only good enough to allow for one year to pass until another sacrifice had to be made for sins. The office of high priest was the one chosen by God so that His people would have someone to make atonement. As good as this was for a season, it was merely a foretaste of what was to come.

That foretaste was pointing to Jesus. In Jesus, we have a great High Priest that did not have to make a yearly sacrifice for sins. He died once for sins, and that was enough to satisfy the requirements of God's righteous law. The writer of Hebrews says, *"he entered once for all into the holy places, not by means of the blood of goats and calves but by means of his own blood, thus securing an eternal redemption." (Hebrews 9:12)* Jesus' blood satisfied God and made propitiation for sins once and for all (1 John 2:2). He is the perfect mediator that we needed to make eternal reconciliation for our sins. *"For there is one God, and there is one mediator between God and men, the man Christ Jesus, who gave himself as a ransom for all, which is the testimony given at the proper time." (1 Timothy 2:5-6)*

When we with think of Christmas, and we think of that baby in the manger, let us worship God because He is the high priest that we still need today. He not only made the sacrifice and stands before God the Father for us, but He was, in fact the sacrifice Himself.

This is the One. Merry Christmas!

December 23rd

The One Who Is King

"Where is he who has been born king of the Jews? For we saw his star when it rose and have come to worship him."
Matthew 2:2

The news that some distant travelers had come to see Him who had been born king of the Jews was all that Herod could stand. He was greatly troubled at their saying and immediately formed a committee to inquire as to where the Messiah was supposed to be born. It was at this point that Herod had begun to plot his demonic scheme. According to Leon Morris, "This Herod is Herod the Great, and he is correctly called 'the king' (the title was sometimes accorded the tetrarch). He was not a Jew, his father being an Idumean and his mother an Arabian, but the Romans made him King of Judea in 40 B.C."[12]

Herod was a prideful and arrogant man who apparently loved his title and position of authority. There was no way that he was going to allow another to take his crown.

---

[12] Leon Morris, *The Gospel according to Matthew*, The Pillar New Testament Commentary (Grand Rapids, MI; Leicester, England: W.B. Eerdmans; Inter-Varsity Press, 1992), 35.

As you now know, there are three Old Testament offices fulfilled by Jesus. The third and final office fulfilled is that of king. Israel first had a king when Saul was anointed (1 Samuel 10). Saul was then rejected by God after he disobeyed by showing partial obedience. (1 Samuel 15) God then anointed David to be the new king of Israel. David was an imperfect king, but he was a king that loved God regardless. David's sons, who reigned in his place, were no better than David. In fact, they were far worse, and led the nation into deep idolatry. There were a few "good" kings that came along here and there, but they were also far from perfect. Having an imperfect king led to having an imperfect nation. This led to the destruction of the nation as the nation was only as close to God as their king was.

God had promised that a king was coming from David's line and that He would be a much different king. The other kings would be blessed as they led the nation in righteousness; however, since they were all unrighteous that would ultimately be an impossible task. Even if a king were a "good" king, the trajectory of the nation depended on, who would take the throne after that king. Instead of getting better, things grew much worse, and God's judgment fell. The kings of Judah and Israel had failed the people.

All of this was to point towards the need for a greater king, a king who would rule with justice, holiness, and lead the people to worship God instead of idols. They would need a king who would lead the people to not live in fear of who might reign next, because this king would reign forever. A king that would not just tell the people to have hearts that worship God, but a king who gives the new heart they would need to obey God fully.

Jesus is this king! He is the one who was to sit on David's throne, and He will reign forever. He is the king that Israel needed then, and He is the king we still need today and forevermore. With Him as king, in the new heavens and new earth, we will never need to fear that His throne will be usurped, that the evil one will win, or that we will sin forever, for He will lead us in righteousness, holiness, and justice. God's people will never be led astray again with Jesus as the King. He is THE King of kings and Lord of lords.

This is the One. Merry Christmas!

Christmas Eve

The One Who Is Worth Sharing

And they went with haste and found Mary and Joseph, and the baby lying in a manger. And when they saw it, they made known the saying that had been told them concerning this child. And all who heard it wondered at what the shepherds told them. - Luke 2:16-18

There is much anticipation leading up to Christmas. There are traditions, parties, events, shopping, cooking, and of course, plans for family to arrive. There is often a lot of hype around the "big day." Usually, when something has a large emotional build up, there inevitably comes an emotional let-down. We often preoccupy ourselves with the hype so that when it's over there is left a void that must be filled. Soon the parties are over, the gifts have been opened, and the decorations have been stored away. Now the reality sets in. Christmas is over until next year, so now what are we to do?

I believe the answer rests partly with the shepherds. The shepherds could not wait to see Him about whom the angels had told them. They went with "haste," meaning that they did not delay. As soon as the heavenly choir of angels stopped their praising of God (Luke 2:13-14), they headed for the manger to find Jesus. I'm sure they talked all the way there about what they would find. Would He really be there? Is this really the One? I'm sure that the adrenaline was pumping all the way to Bethlehem.

When they arrived at the manger, they were not disappointed. They did not hold back the information that they had heard from the angels. *"For unto you is born this day in the city of David a Savior, who is Christ the Lord." (Luke 2:11)* Their news left everyone in amazement. Their awe and wonder soon became everyone else's awe and wonder. Ok, so the party is over, right? Here comes the emotional let-down for the shepherds. They had done their duty and obeyed the voice of the angels.

It was not over for them. When they left, they continued their worship, and I'm sure continued to share the news with many more. *"And the shepherds returned, glorifying and praising God for all they had heard and seen, as it had been told them." (Luke 2:20)*

What if we thought of Christmas a little bit differently than we usually do? What if we don't see it as the end of a celebration but the beginning of one? I believe it would solve many of the

Christmas blues that some feel once the adrenaline and nostalgia pass. The way to do this is by letting Christmas be fuel for your evangelism and worship rather than just a sentimental holiday. In order to be like the Shepherds, we must continue sharing as they did. Why? For Jesus is worth sharing with others.

This is the One. Merry Christmas!

Christmas Day

The One Who Is Worthy of Our Treasuring

But Mary treasured up all these things, pondering them in her heart. - Luke 2:19

Merry Christmas! The day has finally arrived, and if you've been faithful with these readings you have reached the end of our devotional time together. I pray that this brief time together has been fruitful for your life and has made this Christmas season that much more precious to you. Yesterday, I wrote that we must be like the shepherds for they continued to share about the One who was worthy to be shared. Today I will ask you to look at the actions of Mary after she heard the shepherd's announcement. The news that had just been delivered to her about her baby boy left her in great wonder. Luke tells us that this wonder and awe did not cease that night saying, *"But Mary treasured up all these things, pondering them in her heart." (Luke 2:19)* As we conclude this time together, I want you to do what Mary did with the information provided to you about Jesus.

The shepherds had told her very similar things to what the angel had told her about nine months earlier. Mary received the news as confirmation about the identity of her child. The first thing that Mary did was to "treasure" the things told to her by the shepherds. The word treasure in the Greek means to "store up, preserve." Mary did not forget what they had said, but she put them in her memory never to be forgotten. These words were precious to her and she did not want to forget them. I would not be surprised if she found a place to write these words down and then read them from time to time.

Mary did not just store up this information for the sake of storing it up. We tend to keep things just for the sake of keeping them with no intention of ever using them again. Luke tells us that she not only treasured the news, but she also pondered the news. Mary kept reflecting on this glorious announcement and continued to give it some deep, reflective thought. The word "ponder" could also be translated as meditated. Mary treasured and pondered these things because they were precious to her.

This is the reason I wrote this book. I wanted you to know more about the Lord Jesus. I wanted you to focus on and worship Him this Christmas. I wanted those who say, "Jesus is the reason for the season" actually to know what that means. This book has focused on the doctrine of Christology (the study of Christ). I pray that these readings would not just be ones that you cast aside after today as something you only read leading up to Christmas Day. I pray that in the days, weeks, and months ahead that you would treasure and ponder all the things you have read. Who is the Lord Jesus? This book barely begins to scratch the surface. I pray that this has whet your appetite and has given you a new revived fervor for Him.

There are many things that we can treasure and ponder at Christmas. However, there is only One that is worthy of our treasuring. Keep on treasuring. Keep on pondering. Keep on worshipping.

This is the One. Merry Christmas!

.